City Fish
COUNTRY FISH

How Fish Adapt to Tropical Seas and Cold Oceans

MARY M. CERULLO
Photography by Jeffrey L. Rotman

TILBURY HOUSE
PUBLISHERS

Would you be surprised to learn that there are ocean animals that live in the "city" . . .

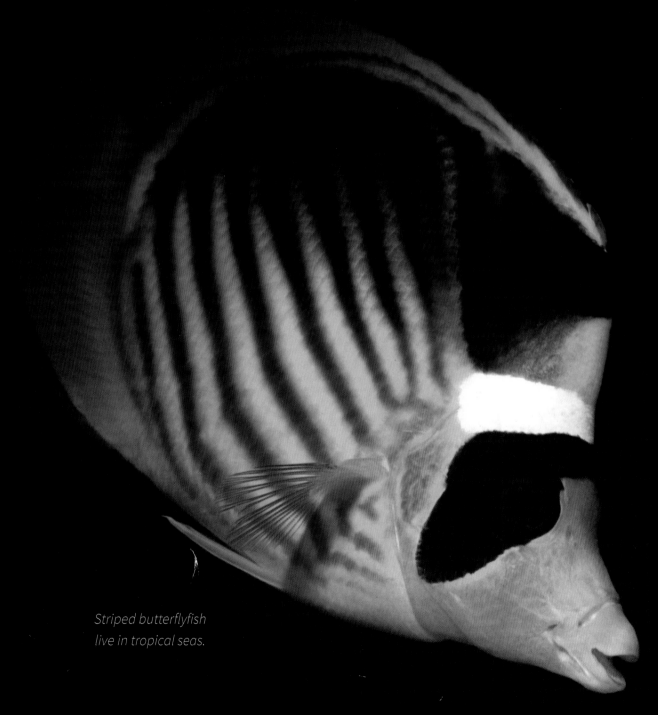

Striped butterflyfish live in tropical seas.

There are zones of life, called *bioregions*, which are determined by their distance from the equator, an imaginary line that circles the middle of the earth. Hugging the equator in areas such as the Caribbean Sea and the Hawaiian Islands are the *tropical* zones, where the waters are warm all year long. *Temperate* regions change with the seasons, and the climate ranges from generally mild, as in Virginia and Maryland, to frosty, as in New England. Waters there are colder. The Arctic and Antarctic are called the *polar* regions. Icebergs and icecaps dot these frigid areas.

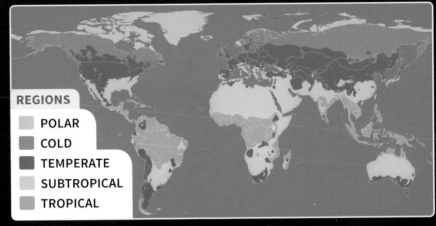

REGIONS

■ POLAR
■ COLD
■ TEMPERATE
■ SUBTROPICAL
■ TROPICAL

A person who lives in Hawaii could switch places with someone who lives in the Arctic Circle (although they may not want to!), but a fish that lives in the tropics would quickly die if it were dumped into the chilly waters of the temperate ocean.

. . . and others that live in the "country"?

Cod live in cold temperate waters.

Tropical reefs are like cities:
DIVERSITY IS ALL AROUND!

Tropical fishes swim in water as warm as a swimming pool.

Exquisite butterflyfish

Masked butterflyfish

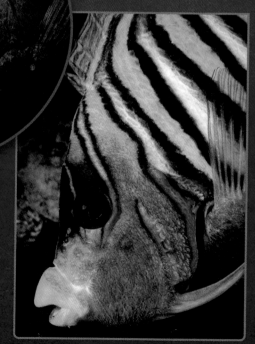

Dusky butterflyfish

Royal angelfish

Their home on a coral reef could be called a city under the sea, because, like a city on land, a coral reef is busy, crowded, and colorful. A single Caribbean coral reef may be home to more than a thousand kinds of plants and animals. A city fish must have "street smarts" to survive. Day or night, it has to defend itself from other fish that would snatch its food, its mate, its hiding place—or the fish itself.

Cold oceans are like the country . . .

Country fish swim in cool waters far from the equator and tropical waters.

Cold-water country fishes such as cod live close to the earth (the ocean floor, actually).

There are not nearly as many kinds of fishes here as in tropical seas—and many of them look pretty much the same. That is not surprising, because several belong to the same family. The cod is the largest member of a family that also includes pollock, haddock, and hake.

The cod fishery is one of the world's largest.

... lots of life but less variety.

Many cold-water fishes travel in giant groups called *schools*. Although this protects them from fish predators, their schooling makes it possible—and profitable—for fishermen to capture thousands of fish at a time.

Pacific mackerel schooling in a giant kelp forest off the Channel Islands of California.

Tropical oceans are BLUE.

The first thing you notice about the tropical ocean is its color: a bright, inviting turquoise. Dive in and you can see deep into the water—below, above, and all around. A city fish may feel as if it can see forever, but even so, it rarely strays far from its home on the coral reef.

School of scalefin anthias

This tiny coral polyp is the foundation of the largest cities on earth: coral reefs.

Like an oasis in the desert, a coral reef provides the only food and shelter for miles around. There are few food particles suspended in the clear water. Any animal that ventures far from the reef is easily spotted by roaming predators.

9

Cold oceans are like GREEN SOUP.

Cold waters are a giant food factory. Minerals washed into the ocean from the land mix with nutritious morsels stirred up from the ocean floor. They become fertilizers for microscopic floating plants. These *phytoplankton* bloom in huge numbers and are eaten by tiny animals called *zooplankton*.

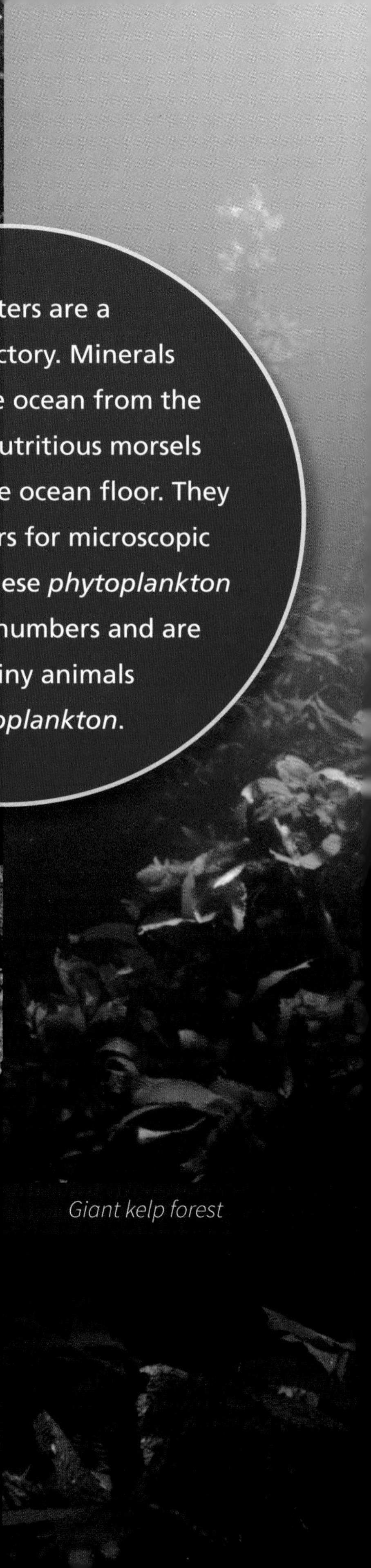

Giant kelp forest

Diver and sea raven

Sunlight overhead in a giant kelp forest

Together, phytoplankton and zooplankton support a huge food web, which includes cod, other fishes, and the animals that eat those fishes.

The phytoplankton near the ocean's surface absorb some of the sun's light, making the water appear green. For much of the year, the water is murky—or, as some would say, "as thick as pea soup." The fishes that live here think of this plankton soup as "dinner."

Rainbow-colored
fishes swim in tropical oceans.

It's not just the color of the water in the tropics that captures your attention. Coral reef fishes brighten the reef with reds, yellows, and blues, and with stripes, spots, and splotches.

No Trespassing! The warning colors on a spotfin lionfish should discourage any attackers.

Royal angelfish

Sergeant majors

Like billboards in the city, eye-catching colors can advertise a message of welcome or of warning. A splash of color can help an angelfish attract a mate, while the deadly lionfish uses its stripes to warn intruders that it's not wise to tangle with the sharp, venomous spines that ripple along its back.

HOW NATURE WORKS

COLORS

It's not easy to find the right balance between being noticed by your friends and becoming a target for your enemies. To solve that problem, a coral reef fish may flash a brilliant color to draw the attention of a female. After a brief encounter, he may quickly change back to a less flashy look. At dusk, the bright colors of some coral reef fishes fade to dark "pajama stripes" as they head off to bed.

Earth-toned fishes
swim in cold oceans.

Sea raven surrounded by metridium anemones

Tiny sacs of pigment called chromatophores stretch or shrink to make the flounder change color.

While city fish often use vivid colors to stand out against their coral reefs, country fish use camouflage, like hunters in the forest, to hide in plain sight. The colors of cold-water fishes are mostly earth tones—tan, brown, and black—that mimic the colors of the seaweeds and rocks on the ocean floor. Those that travel in schools near the ocean's surface tend to have silvery scales that reflect back the light, like waves on water.

Many kinds of fishes can change their skin color to blend in with their surroundings, but the flounder does it best. As it swims across the ocean floor, you can actually watch its color change as it crosses from light sand to dark gravel.

Tropical fishes live in high-rise condos.

A coral reef occupies a relatively small slice of ocean real estate.

It's bounded on one side by land, usually an island or the eastern coast of a continent.

Clownfish

DIVING WHERE IT'S CROWDED AND COLORFUL

Stingrays

When you dive into a coral sea, chances are the reef residents will scatter as you splash into their neighborhood. Once they get used to you, they may reappear. On a calm, sunlit day, you can see for more than 200 feet. What you can't see are the invisible boundaries that fishes set. It might be 3 feet or it might be 80 feet, but they will not allow you to cross that boundary.

You will see an entirely different population of sea creatures if you return to the same reef at night. Your flashlight will reveal shiny eyes in every corner of the reef: squirrelfish, soldierfishes, big-eyed scads, and others. Some fishes, such as grunts and drumfishes, can be heard more than seen, as they make a racket heading off to hunt for prey. Coral polyps extend their stinging tentacles beyond their stony cups to catch tiny plankton floating by or to battle neighboring corals for living space. They use their poison darts to sting, stab, and digest a nextdoor colony of a different species, but only under cover of darkness.

Giant Napoleon wrasse

On the other side, the ocean may drop off sharply into a deep abyss. Since space is tight, there is a lot of competition for hiding places. Even the smallest fishes, with dainty names like angelfish, damselfish, and butterflyfish, are ready to rumble to protect their precious piece of reef.

Like residents in a high-rise apartment building, fishes live at well-defined levels on the coral reef. After a hard day of foraging for food, they return to the same retreats night after night.

Cold-water fishes have ROOM TO ROAM.

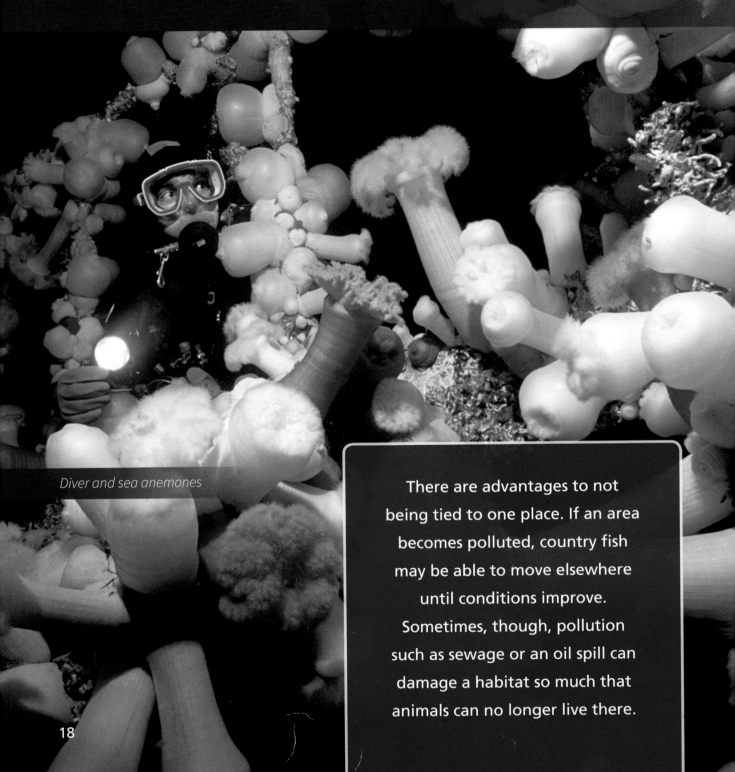

Diver and sea anemones

There are advantages to not being tied to one place. If an area becomes polluted, country fish may be able to move elsewhere until conditions improve. Sometimes, though, pollution such as sewage or an oil spill can damage a habitat so much that animals can no longer live there.

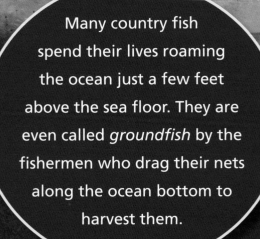

Many country fish spend their lives roaming the ocean just a few feet above the sea floor. They are even called *groundfish* by the fishermen who drag their nets along the ocean bottom to harvest them.

Cod have a special chin whisker called a barbel *for feeling and tasting clams, crabs, and other seafood that lives on the ocean floor.*

DIVING WHERE IT'S MURKY AND MYSTERIOUS

Cold-water diving is also an adventure in many ways. You must wear a wetsuit to stay warm. Sometimes you get so turned around in the murky water that you can't even tell which way is up. You can't see more than 10 feet in any direction, so you won't see multitudes of fish. They sense your presence before you see them, and they stay clear. But you feel a sense of mystery while diving in cold waters; the animals are around you, and you can sense them. For now, humans can only be visitors to the ocean. Whether you visit the "city" or the "country," remember that you are a guest. Be respectful of the residents.

Photographer Jeff Rotman's son Matthew, age 9, encounters a giant 14-pound lobster.

Tropical fishes are FLAT AND COMPACT.

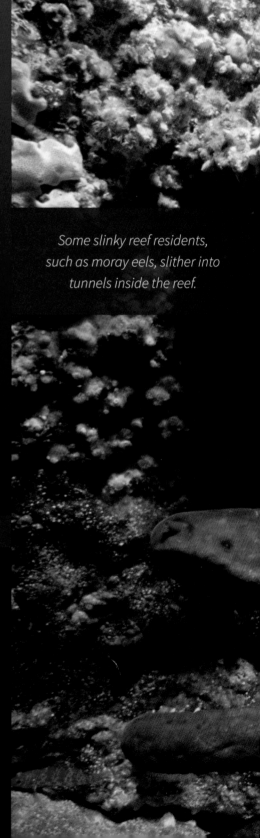

Some slinky reef residents, such as moray eels, slither into tunnels inside the reef.

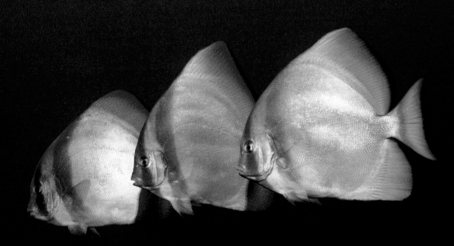

Circular spadefish

Many city fish are not built for long-distance travel since they rarely venture far from the security of their undersea refuges. Instead, coral reef fishes are designed for quick escapes. Many are flattened from side to side like DVDs.

When a scary shadow passes overhead, the fishes dive into hiding places within the coral branches. A large tail and short side fins help them brake and swerve fast, like tiny sports cars.

Cold-water fishes are SOLID AND STURDY.

Skate

A few country fishes are adapted to fit flat against the ocean floor. A skate, the cold-water relative of a stingray, buries itself in sand up to its eyeballs. It breathes through holes in the top of its head called *spiracles*. If it tried to breathe through its mouth, located underneath, it would gulp in a mouthful of sand instead.

But most country
fishes are robust and hardy,
built for swimming long distances.
It's no coincidence that we humans
have designed our underwater
vehicles to resemble the
streamlined, "submarine"
shape of these fishes.

Bluefin tuna are built for speed. Their streamlined shape and long tail fin help make them some of the fastest swimmers in the ocean.

Tropical fishes work together with SYMBIOSIS.

A moray eel will allow a cleaner fish to swim inside its mouth and clean food particles off its teeth.

Unexpected alliances between creatures help to keep a coral reef healthy. When a partnership helps one or both creatures, it is called *symbiosis*, which means "living together." For example, a cleaner fish removes parasites that irritate the skin, mouth, and gills of larger fishes. A customer fish stays still to allow the cleaner to scour its teeth like a diminutive dentist. What do cleaner fish get by performing this good deed? A hearty meal.

The clownfish finds a hiding place inside its symbiotic partner, a sea anemone. In exchange, it lures other fishes into its host's stinging tentacles.

Cold-water fishes work together by SCHOOLING.

Like birds flocking and deer forming herds, these jacks find safety in numbers.

Unlike city fish that huddle in crevices of a coral reef, country fish travel across broad expanses of ocean. They feel safest swimming in the middle of a vast school of other fish.

Being in a school is like being in a huge parade. Fish keep together through sight, sound, and feel. A special organ called the *lateral line* senses the vibrations made by surrounding fish as they move through the water.

Topsmelt silversides

A school of fish has many eyes and other senses to detect predators and locate prey. A predator usually targets one fish within the school. If you were a fish in the middle of a school, chances are that the predator would not choose *you*.

Tropical fishes survive by
SPECIALIZATION.

The parrotfish's teeth have fused together to make a "beak" that can gnaw away at hard coral to get to the tiny plants that live inside.

Orange-spine unicorn fish

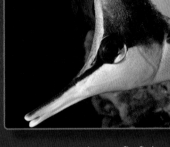

Longnose butterfly fish

All animals have two basic requirements for survival: finding food and avoiding becoming someone else's food. As in our cities on land, there are many kinds of "specialists" doing business on a coral reef, each with its own ways of surviving.

Some coral reef fishes have specialized mouths for getting at just the right meal. The long-nosed butterflyfish has a snout that can poke into narrow openings in the reef to grab tiny shrimp and worms. Other fish have hidden weapons to surprise would-be predators. The surgeonfish has spines as sharp as a surgeon's knife concealed on either side of its tail. These spines spring open the instant the fish senses danger.

Cold-water fishes
survive by HARDINESS.

Amalco jacks

Goosefish

Cold-water fish rely less on specializations and more on strength and stamina. Generally, they use their swimming ability to escape predators and to find food and mates. Many cold-water fishes grow quite large and swim thousands of miles. Migrating fishes need energy and endurance—and the ability to find their way back again.

Unlike some coral reef fish that subsist on a very particular diet, many country fish eat whatever comes their way. With a mouth the size of a garbage can lid, the goosefish eats almost anything it can fit into its mouth. It lures flounder, lobsters, and sea snails with a wriggling "worm" that is actually a piece of its own skin. Goosefish sometimes grab ducks or gulls resting on the ocean surface. (So far, it's never been proven that goosefish have eaten geese!)

A coral reef
NEVER SLEEPS.

Like a city, a coral reef is bustling both day and night. Animals that live on different schedules sometimes share the same shelter within the reef. Like factory workers, they may pass each other as they change shifts.

Over half the reef fishes work the "day shift." Their sharp eyes and quick reflexes help them evade danger as they search for food.

As daylight fades, the daytime fishes cannot see as clearly. They drift closer to the safety of branching corals, wary of predators that may lurk in the shadows.

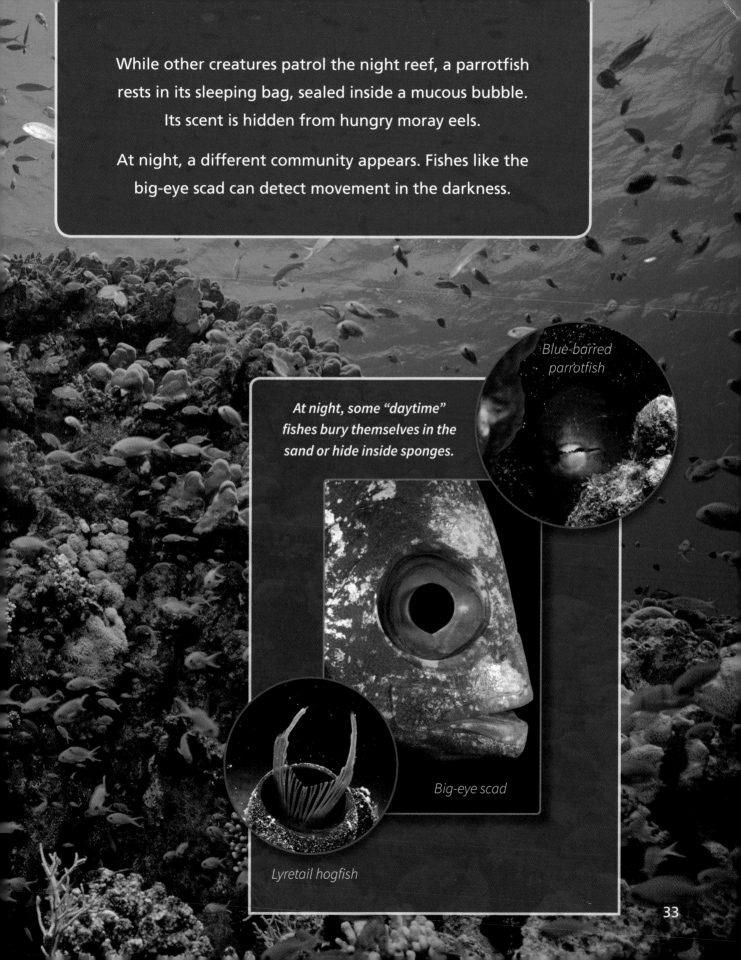

While other creatures patrol the night reef, a parrotfish rests in its sleeping bag, sealed inside a mucous bubble. Its scent is hidden from hungry moray eels.

At night, a different community appears. Fishes like the big-eye scad can detect movement in the darkness.

At night, some "daytime" fishes bury themselves in the sand or hide inside sponges.

Blue-barred parrotfish

Big-eye scad

Lyretail hogfish

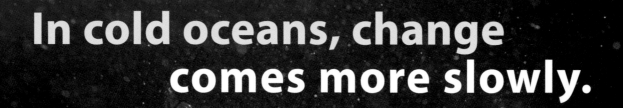

In cold oceans, change comes more slowly.

The rhythm of life is slower in cold waters. Changes here happen over 365 days rather than 24 hours.

Cunners

California sheephead, kelp bass, and garibaldi in kelp forest

Giant kelp

Groundfishing

The cycle of life is tied to the changing seasons. In spring, longer days with more sunlight set the stage for rebirth. The first crop of phytoplankton blooms in early spring, followed by another bloom in late summer. As if on cue, tiny animals such as baby crabs, fish, and lobsters hatch to take advantage of the sudden surge in food supply.

Sharks roam the reefs . . .

At dawn and dusk on the coral reef, unwelcome guests show up like uninvited relatives at a family reunion.

Whitetip reef shark

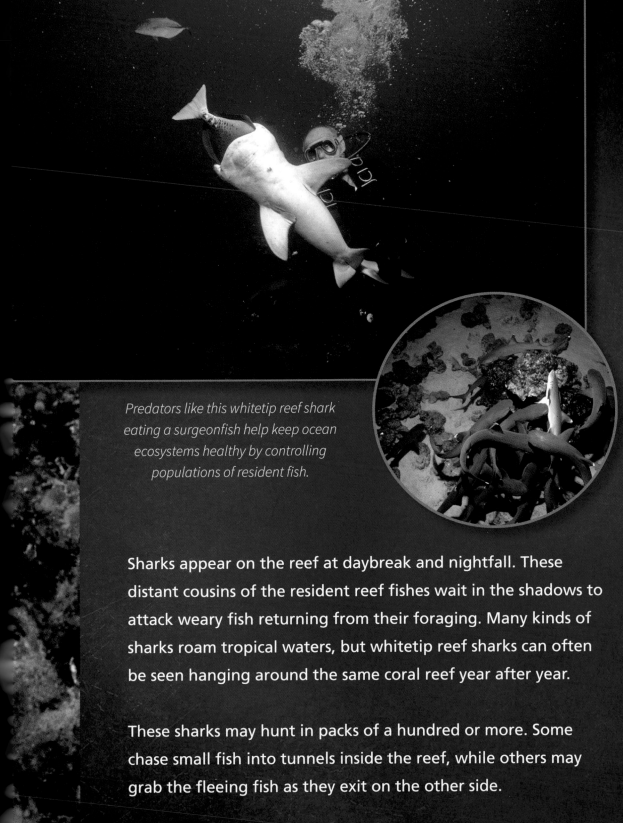

Predators like this whitetip reef shark eating a surgeonfish help keep ocean ecosystems healthy by controlling populations of resident fish.

Sharks appear on the reef at daybreak and nightfall. These distant cousins of the resident reef fishes wait in the shadows to attack weary fish returning from their foraging. Many kinds of sharks roam tropical waters, but whitetip reef sharks can often be seen hanging around the same coral reef year after year.

These sharks may hunt in packs of a hundred or more. Some chase small fish into tunnels inside the reef, while others may grab the fleeing fish as they exit on the other side.

Great white shark

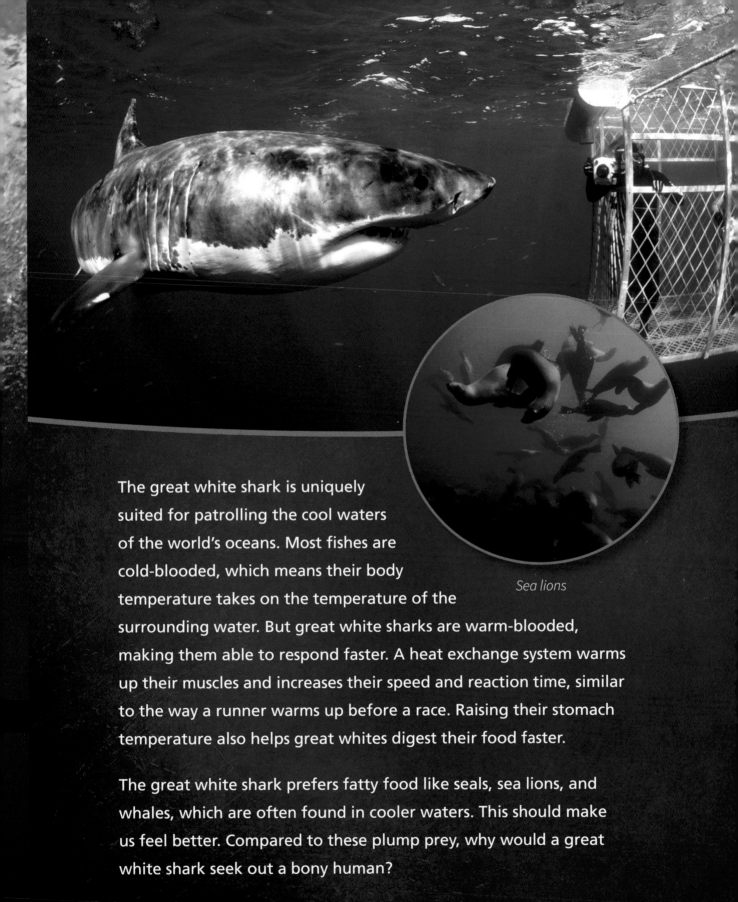

Sea lions

The great white shark is uniquely suited for patrolling the cool waters of the world's oceans. Most fishes are cold-blooded, which means their body temperature takes on the temperature of the surrounding water. But great white sharks are warm-blooded, making them able to respond faster. A heat exchange system warms up their muscles and increases their speed and reaction time, similar to the way a runner warms up before a race. Raising their stomach temperature also helps great whites digest their food faster.

The great white shark prefers fatty food like seals, sea lions, and whales, which are often found in cooler waters. This should make us feel better. Compared to these plump prey, why would a great white shark seek out a bony human?

Fish, like us, are all the same
—but different.

It's been fun to think of ways that tropical reefs are like "cities" and cooler waters are more "country," but it is important to remember that this comparison is only a way to explore ocean diversity. Fishes everywhere share many common traits.

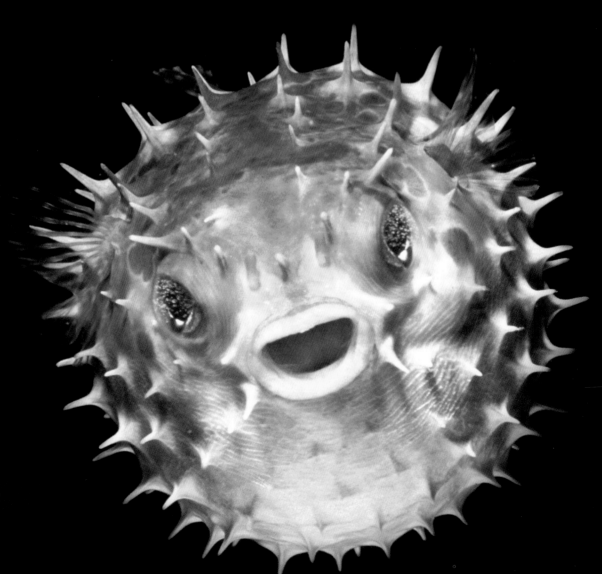

Pufferfish

Red-lipped batfish

Spiny sea horse

Sapphire gurnard

We sometimes see brightly colored fishes in temperate waters, and you can find schools of fishes in the tropics. In reality, there is a little bit of country and a little bit of city in the animals that live in both regions.

Swordfish (shown here) and tuna can sprint through the water at speeds approaching 80 kilometers an hour (50 mph).

Most fishes share characteristics that make them FISH. They have gills for taking oxygen from the water and a lateral line for sensing vibrations underwater. They have fins for swimming, turning, or staying upright in the water. Most fishes also have an organ called a *swim bladder*, which can inflate or deflate like a balloon to keep them at a certain level in the ocean. But some fishes don't fit the mold. Why are certain fishes designed the way they are? What good are "legs" (actually, they're modified side fins) on a sea robin? Why does a red-lipped batfish look like it's wearing lipstick? Why are sea horses shaped like a question mark? Making educated guesses based on a fish's habits and habitat is what *ichthyologists* do.

studying bonnethead sharks

41

The ocean is
CHANGING.

Pink clownfish in sea anemone

We hear a lot about how climate change is affecting Earth, as carbon dioxide (from smokestacks and tailpipes) and other "greenhouse gases" become trapped in the upper atmosphere. Climate change is blamed for record warm temperatures, wild weather, and sea level rises that are flooding coastal properties.

But how is climate change affecting the oceans?

As we've learned, coral polyps are the foundation of our planet's vast coral reefs. Within the polyps live tiny, single-celled organisms—*zooxanthellae*—that help the coral grow. Zooxanthellae also create the colors of the living reef. When the water gets too warm, these tiny algae cells can swim away, exposing the white skeletons of the corals. If conditions improve, they may return. If not, the reef dies. Eventually, the dead coral becomes covered in a fuzzy blanket of green algae.

Anemone fish in the Celebes Sea of Indonesia

Coral reefs are also suffering from another assault—increasingly acidic water—that can dissolve coral and other sea creatures made of calcium carbonate. This is called *ocean acidification*. What causes it? Scientists say that up to a third of all the carbon dioxide released by the burning of coal, oil, and gas is absorbed by the oceans. What's more, when rainwater washes from the land, it flushes sewage, pet waste, and fertilizers into coastal waters. These pollutants can trigger blooms of tiny ocean plants—phytoplankton—and when these phytoplankton die, their decay uses up oxygen and produces more carbon dioxide. More carbon dioxide means more carbonic acid and a more acidic ocean.

A one-year-old American lobster

Scientists predict that over time, many coral reefs may stop growing and eventually erode away. Thousands of sea creatures will lose their oases in the tropical oceanic desert.

Meanwhile, even cold waters are getting warmer, favoring the growth of less nourishing plankton for animals higher up the food chain. Instead of nutritious copepods and krill, some sea creatures may have to subsist on "junk food" like salps and jellies.

OCEAN ACIDIFICATION

What is ocean acidification? When water and carbon dioxide mix, they form a weak acid called *carbonic acid*. This is the acid that, under pressure, provides the fizz in soft drinks and carbonated water. As it drips through caves, carbonic acid dissolves limestone to create stalactites and stalagmites. And when it accumulates in seawater, it can cause sea shells and coral to dissolve.

Bleached cor...

Those who grow seafood such as oysters have already seen their "crops" ... from higher acidity. The shells of animals like mussels, scallops, clams, and o... may become pitted and even dissolve. Baby lobsters put into aquarium tanks ... high levels of carbon dioxide grow more slowly and molt less often than lobst... normal seawater.

Much of what we know so far comes from laboratory experiments. It's harder to ... what is happening in the ocean, but we do know that many sea creatures are al... being affected. Scientists estimate that up to 90 percent of sea life will eventua... impacted by warming water, rising sea level, and more acidic conditions. Researcher... harvesters are experimenting with growing sea grasses and kelp to take up the nut... that produce excess carbon dioxide, and spreading crushed shells on clam flats to b... the acidity (like taking an antacid to buffer a sour stomach). Some scientists are cultiv... species of corals that can tolerate more acidic conditions. What can we do to help?

- Bike or walk instead of asking for a ride.

- Don't waste energy! Turn off lights when you leave a room. Don't let the ... run when you are brushing your teeth. Start the dishwasher and washing machine only when you have a full load.

- Pick up pet poop and put it in the toilet or garbage can.

Simple actions like these *do* make a difference.

The Ocean is a GREAT PLACE TO LIVE!

Seargeant majors

Purple anthias

Rays

How many fishes are in the ocean? Estimates range from 14,000 to 28,000 species, but those are just guesses. Chances are there are many more fishes out there that we don't even know about yet.

Tropical reef fishes live in clear, warm waters that show off their bright colors and special adaptations. Cold-water fishes swim through a feast of plankton-rich waters. Their differences help them survive in their part of the ocean.

Those differences make the ocean a better place to live. That huge variety—what scientists call "diversity"—is important for maintaining the health of the oceans.

A healthy ocean isn't just important to fishes; a healthy ocean is important to us people. Not only does the ocean provide half the oxygen we breathe, it affects our weather, challenges our skills, and nurtures our spirits.

Fishes face dangers that they cannot control—but we can. Fish can't protect their communities from pollution, overfishing, and climate change. For that, they must rely on the kindness of strangers—people who work to protect the world's oceans.

School of barracuda

Moray eel

After all, city or country, fishes or people, above or below the waves—

It's all one world

Glossary

abyss: a deep canyon in the ocean with straight walls

barbel: a whiskerlike projection on the lower jaw of certain fishes, such as catfish and cod

bioregion: an area with the required range of temperatures and other environmental conditions that certain animals and plants need to survive

camouflage: any kind of coloring that helps an animal blend with its surroundings

chromatophore: a tiny sac of pigment that stretches or shrinks to make an animal change color

cold-blooded: a condition in an animal, such as a fish or a reptile, in which its body temperature changes with the temperature of the surrounding environment

diversity: variety in nature; many different kinds of plants, animals, and habitats help an ecosystem resist or recover quickly from diseases, pollution, and other disturbances

ecosystem: how living things and their environment function as a unit

equator: an imaginary line around the middle of the earth that divides the northern and southern hemispheres

food web: the complex relationship of who eats whom in a community

groundfish: a fish that spends most of its life swimming near the ocean floor

ichthyologist: a scientist who studies fish

lateral line: a line of sensory organs along the length of a fish that detect vibrations in the water

nutrient: a nourishing substance

phytoplankton microscopic plants that drift on the current; literally, "wanderers"

polar: relating to, connected with, or located near the North Pole or South Pole

polyp: the nonswimming stage of a coral or a sea anemone, shaped like a hollow cup with tentacles surrounding the open end

spiracles: small openings on either side of a skate or ray's eyes, where water is drawn in and then passed over its gills

swim bladder: an organ that inflates or deflates with gas to keep fish at a certain level in the water

symbiosis: when two different species live together, and at least one benefits

temperate: describing an area that is moderate in temperature; although seasonal changes are apparent, it is not subject to prolonged extremes of hot or cold weather

tropical: an area that is warm year-round, typically near or on the equator

warm-blooded: a condition in an animal, such as a shark or a mammal, in which its body temperature stays the same regardless of the temperature of the surrounding environment

year class: the year in which a group of fish is born, which identifies them for the rest of their lives; the term is typically used by scientists and fishermen to describe when fish can be harvested

zooxanthellae: single-celled photosynthetic algae that live in reef-building coral polyps

zooplankton: small, drifting animals that feed on phytoplankton or other zooplankton; sometimes the baby stages of animals such as fish and crabs

Fish or Fishes?

Scientists use *fish* as a plural to describe a number of fish of the same kind, or species; they use *fishes* when they are talking about several different kinds, such as the variety of fishes one might find on a coral reef.

Diving Deeper

The Cod's Tale, Mark Kurlansky (New York: G.P. Putnam's Sons, 2001)

Swimmy, Leo Lionni (New York: Pantheon Books, 1963)

Shark Expedition: A Shark Photographer's Close Encounters, Mary M. Cerullo (North Mankato, MN: Compass Point Books, 2015)

The Truth about Dangerous Marine Animals, Mary M. Cerullo (San Francisco: Chronicle, 2003)

Sea Soup: Phytoplankton, Mary M. Cerullo (Gardiner, Maine: Tilbury House, 1999)

Sea Soup: Zooplankton, Mary M. Cerullo (Gardiner, Maine: Tilbury House, 2001)

Surrounded by Sea: Life on a New England Fishing Island, Gail Gibbons (Boston: Little, Brown, 1991)

MARY CERULLO has written more than 20 nonfiction books on ocean life for children, including *Sharks* (a *School Library Journal* Best Book of the Year), *Octopus* (a Junior Library Guild Selection), *Giant Squid* (an Outstanding Science Trade Book selection by the National Science Teachers Association and the Children's Book Council), and *The Truth About White Sharks* (IRA Teacher's Choice Award). In her day job, Mary is the associate director of Friends of Casco Bay, an environmental group on the Gulf of Maine.

JEFFREY ROTMAN started taking pictures of ocean animals to capture the attention of his middle-school students, and eventually gave up teaching to devote himself to underwater photography. His work has been featured on television, in many successful books, and in *Life, Time, Smithsonian, The New York Times, National Geographic, Geo, Stern, Paris Match, Le Figaro*, and other publications. He has been named the BBC "Underwater Wildlife Photographer of the Year."

Tilbury House Publishers
12 Starr St.
Thomaston, Maine 04861
800–582–1899 • www.tilburyhouse.com

Second edition: March 2017 • 10 9 8 7 6 5 4 3 2 1

Dedications:
For the one with the sea and sky in her name: Taylor Marina Cerullo —MMC
For my favorite dive buddies: Matthew and Thomas Rotman —JLR

Acknowledgments:
Many thanks to: Dr. John Annala, formerly Chief Scientific Officer, Gulf of Maine Research Institute and Chief Scientist, New Zealand Ministry of Fisheries; Brian Tarbox, Professor of Marine Science, Southern Maine Community College, and author Ron Hirschi, for reviewing the final text.

Thanks also to Wayne Bruzek for working his artistic magic with the photographs; Isabelle Delafosse for helping to select the images in this book; and Karen Fisk for her encouragement. I am also grateful to Jeff Rotman, who with over forty years' experience diving with fishes, contributed his unique insight to the text of this book. Any errors are the author's alone.

Library of Congress Control Number: 2016959413

Cover and interior design by Frame25 Productions
Printed in Shenzhen, China, by Shenzhen Caimei Printing Co., Ltd.,
through Four Colour Print Group, Louisville, KY

Production Date: December 2016
Batch Number: 68213-0
Plant Location Shenzhen, China

HOW NATURE WORKS books don't just catalog the natural world in beautiful photographs. They seek to understand why nature functions as it does. They ask questions, and they encourage readers to ask more. They explore nature's mysteries, sharing what we know and celebrating what we have yet to discover. Other HOW NATURE WORKS books include:

Catching Air: Taking the Leap with Gliding Animals

978-0-8848-496-7

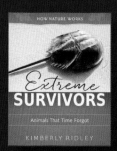

Extreme Survivors: Animals That Time Forgot

978-0-88448-500-1